YOUR KNOWLEDGE HAS VALUE

Marlene Weber

"Frankenstein" von Mary Shelley. Analyse einer Passage

Frankenstein or the Modern Prometheus, 1818 Text

GRIN Verlag

Bibliografische Information der Deutschen Nationalbibliothek:

Die Deutsche Bibliothek verzeichnet diese Publikation in der Deutschen National-
bibliografie; detaillierte bibliografische Daten sind im Internet über http://dnb.d-
nb.de/ abrufbar.

Imprint:

Copyright © 2012 GRIN Verlag GmbH
Druck und Bindung: Books on Demand GmbH, Norderstedt Germany
ISBN: 978-3-656-55806-4

This book at GRIN:

http://www.grin.com/en/e-book/266075/frankenstein-von-mary-shelley-analyse-
einer-passage

GRIN - Your knowledge has value

Der GRIN Verlag publiziert seit 1998 wissenschaftliche Arbeiten von Studenten, Hochschullehrern und anderen Akademikern als eBook und gedrucktes Buch. Die Verlagswebsite www.grin.com ist die ideale Plattform zur Veröffentlichung von Hausarbeiten, Abschlussarbeiten, wissenschaftlichen Aufsätzen, Dissertationen und Fachbüchern.

Visit us on the internet:

http://www.grin.com/

http://www.facebook.com/grincom

http://www.twitter.com/grin_com

Ludwig-Maximilians-Universität München

Department für Anglistik und Amerikanistik

Wintersemester 2012/2013

Proseminar: Einführung in die Literaturwissenschaft

Second Assignment

Frankenstein

Marlene Weber

Lehramt Realschule, Englisch - Geschichte

1. Semester

The passage provided from M. Shelley´s *Frankenstein* is a part of Victor Frankenstein´s description of the journey he and his friend Henry Clerval undertake, after the monster killed his brother William and demanded Victor to create a female companion. In particular, it is a description of the stay in Oxford and Victor´s inner thoughts and feelings.

He describes the city of Oxford very pictorially. The reader gets the impression that this is the perfect city ("[...] its majestic assemblage of towers, spires, and domes, [...]", l 4f) and the best place for Victor´s "miserable [...] self" (l 15f) to recover; as he says at the end of the passage "my soul was elevated" (l 23). Although he has the monster and its demand for a companion in the back of his mind, he is a little bit calmer and less nervous as he usually is, as there are no exclamations or questions. Instead of short and snatchy sentences, he uses long ones which make the stream of speech smooth and steady (e.g. l 1-5, l 17-22).

Throughout the text, Victor uses – on the one hand - numerous positive words to describe Oxford, his surroundings and when he talks about the English history. There are words such as "magnificent" (l 2), "enjoyment" (l 6), "peaceful happiness" (l 8); expressions like "my soul was elevated" (l 23) or even "a free and lofty spirit" (l 27). He seems to enjoy the journey together with his best friend. However, in the whole book, such words are used very rarely by Victor. He is constantly terrorized by his creation and is also very depressed, especially since the time when the monster begins to murder his family. This is very well mirrored in the usage of – on the other hand- various negative words and expressions such as "embittered" (l 6), "wrecked" (l 15), "debasing and miserable fears" (l 23 f); he even says "[...] the iron had eaten into my flesh [...]" (l 27f) when he compares his problems with "chains" (l 26).

Generally, the positive words are mainly used for nature, voyages, Victor´s family, science and the past (especially his childhood); while the negative words are mostly used for his inner condition and memories, e.g. the guilt and fear he feels when thinking upon his creation: "But I am a blasted tree; the bolt has entered my soul; [...]" (l 13). Like the bolt entered the tree, the creation and existence of the monster enters his soul and in the end, destroys Victor. This oppositeness of positive and negative words in this passage is just another example of the basic conflict between good and bad in the whole book. This antagonism can be interpreted in different ways. First, as I mentioned above, *good* can stand for the outside world (nature, travelling, family and friends, learning and science, Victor´s childhood) and *bad* for his inside world (irrevocable mistake of creating the monster, Victor´s carelessness about it, he keeps it as a secret, his guilt for the murder of William as well as his fear that the monster fulfils its threat to kill the rest of his family). Secondly the antagonism, of course, portrays the conflict between Victor and his creation. Ever since the monster was created, its existence is a constant threat which he tries to ignore, for example when he says:

"For an instant I dared to shake off my chains, and look around me with a free and lofty spirit; but the iron had eaten into my flesh, and I sank again, trembling and hopeless, into my miserable self" (l 26 ff).

These are the most important lines in this passage. They once again emphasize Victor´s inner conflict and there are again many positive as well as negative expressions. On the one hand, they show the pressure and tension, his guilt, fear and hopelessness. On the other hand, it reveals that he tries to ignore all this from time to time and seeks distraction from his misery (e.g. when he is travelling with his friend).

However, there is also a similarity among all the contradictions mentioned above. Victor and the monster both are not bad from the very beginning. Victor has a lovely childhood and when he comes to Ingolstadt, he is eager to learn and improve in the sciences. When he dares to create life, he realizes his hybris. He has a bad conscience towards his creation as he does not care about it and even after it killed William, he thinks about creating a female companion for it. Victor only gives up his life when Elizabeth is murdered. From this point onwards his only aim is to seek revenge and kill the monster. It is the same with his creation. After it left Ingolstadt, it tries several times to get in contact with humans, especially with the De Lacey family. It is rejected; people flee from it in anxiety. After it fails with the De Laceys, it begins to hate all humans and swears revenge.